Rites of Passage

Funerals

Mandy Ross

Heinemann
LIBRARY

H **www.heinemann.co.uk/library**

Visit our website to find out more information about **Heinemann Library** books.

To order:

☎ Phone 44 (0) 1865 888066

▤ Send a fax to 44 (0) 1865 314091

▢ Visit the Heinemann Bookshop at www.heinemann.co.uk/library to browse our catalogue and order online.

First published in Great Britain by Heinemann Library, Halley Court, Jordan Hill, Oxford OX2 8EJ, part of Harcourt Education. Heinemann is a registered trademark of Harcourt Education Ltd.

Editorial: Jilly Attwood and Claire Throp
Design: David Poole and Geoff Ward
Picture Research: Rosie Garai and Su Alexander
Production: Séverine Ribierre

Originated by Ambassador Litho Ltd
Printed in China by W K T

ISBN 0 431 17712 0 (hardback)
07 06 05 04 03
10 9 8 7 6 5 4 3 2 1

ISBN 0 431 17719 8 (paperback)
08 07 06 05 04
10 9 8 7 6 5 4 3 2 1

British Library Cataloguing in Publication Data
Ross, Mandy
Funerals - (Rites of Passage)
393
A full catalogue record for this book is available from the British Library.

Acknowledgements
The publishers would like to thank the following for permission to reproduce photographs:
Alamy pp. **17**, **24** (Christine Osborne); Christine Osborne pp. **12**, **16**, **19**; Christine Osborne/Syder p. **20**; Corbis pp. **6** (Richard T. Nowitz), **7** (David Rubinger), **10** (Wolfgang Kaehler), **21** (Najlah Feanny), **25** (Philip Gould), **28** (Phil Schermeister); Getty Images p. **4** (Terry Vine); Impact pp. **5, 8** (Mohamed Ansar), **14** (Christophe Bluntzer), **15** (Mark Henley), **18** (Robin Laurance) **26** (Mark Cator); Lonely Planet Images p. **11** (Dennis Johnson); Magnum pp. **9** (Thomas Dworzak), **27** (Harry Gruyaert); Photofusion p. **29** (Mo Wilson); Rex Features p. **13**; South American Pictures pp. **22**, **23**

Cover photograph of a Buddhist funeral procession near Hanoi, Vietnam, reproduced with permission of Corbis/Owen Franken.

The publishers would like to thank both the Interfaith Education Centre, Bradford and Georga Godwin for their assistance in the preparation of this book.

Every effort has been made to contact copyright holders of any material reproduced in this book. Any omissions will be rectified in subsequent printings if notice is given to the publishers.

Contents

Why do we have funerals?   4

Jewish funerals   6

Muslim funerals   8

Maori funerals   10

Christian funerals   12

Buddhist funerals   14

Sikh funerals   16

Hindu funerals   18

Air and sea burials   20

Remembering the dead   22

Dancing at funerals   24

Ancestor worship   26

New and old traditions   28

Glossary   30

Further resources   31

Index   32

Any words printed in bold letters, **like these**,
are explained in the Glossary.

Why do we have funerals?

A funeral is a special **ritual** or gathering held when someone dies. It lets relatives and friends express their love for the person who has died, and their sadness at his or her death. After the funeral, the dead person's body is usually either buried under the ground or **cremated**.

At a funeral, there are two main jobs to do: to take care of the body and the spirit, or **soul**, of the person who has died, and to look after the needs of the living people left behind.

In every culture around the world, funerals and special rituals are carried out when someone dies. Rituals may include washing and dressing the dead person's body, a **procession** taking the body to the place of burial or cremation, and celebrating the life of the person who has died.

Flowers are often put on a coffin to show love for the person who has died.

Rites of passage

In 1909, a man called Arnold van Gennep wrote about rites of passage, which mark important moments of change in a person's life. He said there are three changes in every rite of passage:

- leaving one group
- moving on to a new stage
- and joining a new group.

What happens to us after we die?

In some religions, people believe that a new life begins after death, in heaven or close to God. Other religions teach about **reincarnation**, which is the belief that a dead person's spirit starts a new life within another living being. Some people believe that death is simply the end of life.

These different beliefs affect traditions for dealing with the body. For example, most people who believe in reincarnation see the body as something that is no longer needed after death and so cremation is used rather than burial.

This book is organized so that funerals based on burial traditions are grouped together, followed by funerals based on cremation, and then other traditions.

This is a procession to a funeral in French Guyana, South America.

Jewish funerals

Jewish funerals take place as soon as possible after someone has died, usually within 24 hours. According to tradition, most **Jews** are buried after they die, although some Jewish people nowadays choose **cremation** instead.

The dead person's body is washed and dressed in a white **shroud**. The body is placed in a simple coffin, the same for everyone, rich or poor. This shows that everyone is equal before God. Someone stays with the coffin until the funeral, to show respect for the person who has died.

A rabbi (Jewish religious leader) says prayers with the family at home before the burial. At the burial ground, the rabbi, relatives and friends say **memorial** prayers and readings from the Hebrew Bible, the Jewish **holy** book. The rabbi speaks about the person who has died, celebrating their life and achievements.

These men are Orthodox Jews praying round the grave in a Jewish cemetery. An Orthodox Jew is one who follows the laws of Judaism strictly.

A gravestone in a Jewish cemetery. The writing is in Hebrew, the language of Jewish prayer. The gravestone is set up to a year after the death, to mark the end of the time of mourning.

For seven days after a death, the family stay at home to **mourn** the dead person. This is called 'sitting Shivah'. Relatives and friends visit for prayers every evening. On the anniversary of the death each year, the dead person's name is read out at the synagogue (the Jewish place of worship), and relatives light a special candle, called a yahrzeit (say 'YART-site') candle, which burns for 24 hours.

Mandy's story

Mandy, who is Jewish, remembers her uncle's funeral:

'*Our rabbi led the funeral prayers and talked about how my uncle had been a good man. Afterwards, we sat Shivah at home for him. He had so many friends and relatives, and they all came to celebrate his memory and comfort our family.*'

Muslim funerals

When a **Muslim** is dying, he or she will try to say the Shahadah, a special prayer that declares faith in God, or Allah. When someone has died, it is traditional for Muslims to say, 'To Allah we belong and to Him is our return'. Both these show the importance of Allah's will.

Muslim families are sad at losing someone they love, but they are comforted by their faith. Muslims believe that the **soul** will go to Paradise after death, if the person has lived his or her life according to Allah's law, which is expressed in the Qur'an (say 'kor-ARN'), the Muslim **holy** book.

These men are carrying a coffin in a funeral procession in Pakistan.

After death, everyone is treated the same, to show that everyone is equal before Allah. The dead person's body is washed and then dressed in white cloth. The cloth may have been worn by the person when they went on **pilgrimage**, or hajj. The funeral and burial are usually held as soon as possible after the person's death. The body is taken in a coffin to a mosque (Muslim place of worship) for prayers, often inside the prayer hall itself. The prayers are usually led by close male relatives or friends.

Muslims bury their dead, rather than using **cremation**, because Allah said that humans should not use fire to destroy what Allah has created. A Muslim is buried in a Muslim cemetery, lying on his or her right side, facing towards the holy city of Makkah. (During their lives, Muslims face in this direction when they pray.) Family members may come and visit the grave, especially at the festival of Id-ul-Fitr.

These **mourners** *are attending the funeral of a young child in Pakistan.*

Maori funerals

Maori people live in the land now called New Zealand. Their **ancestors** lived there for many hundreds of years before the Europeans arrived. According to ancient tradition, Maoris believe that after someone dies, their **spirit** lives on and is cared for by the spirits of earlier ancestors. Maoris believe that their ancestors' spirits live on at the traditional meeting place, called the marae (say 'ma-ray'). They believe that the spirits watch and take part in tribal meetings, marriages, funerals and other ceremonies held at the marae.

When someone dies, his or her body is perfumed and dressed in fine clothes. Then the body is brought to the marae. People gather there to pay their respects to the person who has died. The women of the tribe call to welcome the dead person's spirit and to help it on its journey to meet the spirits. Family and friends wail and cry loudly, to express their sorrow – and so that the soul of the dead person can hear their grief.

A marae, or traditional Maori meeting place, at Rotorua, New Zealand.

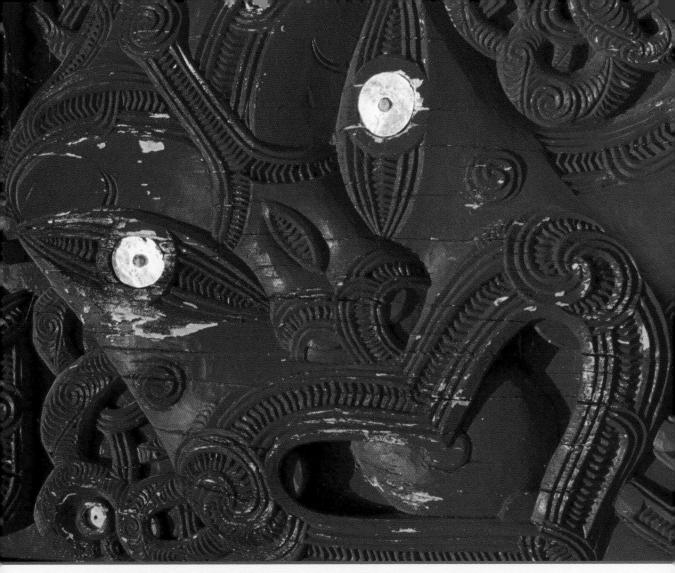

A Maori carving called the Tiki. It is believed to have been carved in memory of an ancestor who died long ago.

On the night before the burial, everyone gathers to sing songs and to remember the dead. They tell stories and look forward to the time when they themselves will meet their loved ones again, after they die.

Then the dead person's body is buried in the family grave. Afterwards, there is a feast for family and friends, and the house is blessed so that the dead person's spirit will not hover over it. A **memorial** stone is placed over the grave within five years of the burial.

Christian funerals

Christians believe that Jesus Christ started a new life in heaven after he died on the cross. So Christians hope that, if they lead a good life, their **soul**, or spirit, will start a new life close to God in heaven after death. When a Christian is dying, the priest or minister may be called to say last prayers with him or her, to help the soul travel quickly to heaven.

The dead person's body is placed in a coffin. Sometimes relatives or friends watch over it before the funeral.

At the funeral, it is traditional to wear dark clothes. There are prayers and readings from the Bible, the Christian **holy** book, and hymns are often sung. Family and friends may talk about their memories of the person who has died, and celebrate their life.

*An elaborate, traditional funeral **procession** in London, UK. The coffin is placed inside the hearse, which is being pulled by horses here.*

It is traditional for a coffin to be carried into the church or crematorium. Sometimes relatives of the person who has died carry the coffin.

Many Christians, especially **Roman Catholics** and **Orthodox** Christians, wish to be buried after they die. If the funeral takes place in a church, then they may be buried in the graveyard beside the church, or else in a public cemetery.

Other Christians choose to be **cremated** instead. Then the funeral is held in the crematorium (where cremation takes place), usually beside a cemetery. After the cremation, the ashes are collected and placed in a special **urn**. Some families scatter the ashes later in a favourite place. Others keep the ashes at home or in a special part of the cemetery.

For some Christians, such as Roman Catholics, it is traditional to hold a party just after the funeral, so that family and friends can gather together to celebrate the life of the person who has died. This brings comfort in a sad time, and reminds the **mourners** that their own life must continue, despite their grief.

Buddhist funerals

Buddhists believe in **reincarnation** – that is, they believe that death is the beginning of a new life. A dead person's **spirit** is born again as another living person or as an animal. Of course relatives and friends feel sad at losing a loved one. But Buddhists see death as part of a natural cycle. Many Buddhists choose to be **cremated**, just as the Buddha, their teacher, was cremated.

This is a traditional pyre for a Buddhist funeral in Bali.

When a Buddhist dies, his or her body is washed and dressed, and then placed in an open coffin. Monks may visit the family to chant from the Buddhist **holy** writings.

The dead person's body is taken in a **procession** to the crematorium, where the cremation takes place. At the funeral there is more chanting, to help the dead person's spirit on its journey. Relatives offer flowers and sweet-smelling **incense** to the Buddha.

The day after the cremation, the ashes are collected and may be kept in an **urn**. Family and friends gather to chant prayers after seven days, and for seven weeks after the death. Buddhists give food and money to the poor, and to the monks after someone has died. They do the same every year on the anniversary of the person's death.

A funeral gathering at a Buddhist temple in China.

Janaki's story

Janaki, a Buddhist from Sri Lanka, remembers attending her grandmother's funeral when she was twelve:

'My grandmother's body was carried to the cemetery near her home. There the coffin was placed on a pyre built of bamboo and decorated with coconut leaves and white tissue paper. I was so sad, I cried and cried. But we hoped that her next life would be happy and good.'

Sikh funerals

Sikhs believe in transmigration. This means that after a person dies their **soul** passes into another body. The person who has died is **cremated** because Sikhs believe that the soul has no more use for the body.

Funerals are the same for everyone, rich and poor, because everyone is seen as equal within the Sikh religion.

The dead person's body is washed and dressed in white. Baptised Sikhs will wear the traditional Sikh **symbols**, the Five Ks: *kesh* (uncut hair), *kangha* (wooden comb), *kara* (steel bracelet), *kirpan* (symbolic sword), and *kachera* (cotton undershorts). Then the dead person's body is brought home for family and friends to say goodbye. At home, the family reads from the Sikh **holy** book, called the Siri Guru Granth Sahib (say 'si-ree goo-roo gran-th sar-hib').

These Sikhs are saying goodbye to a dead relative. An open coffin is used.

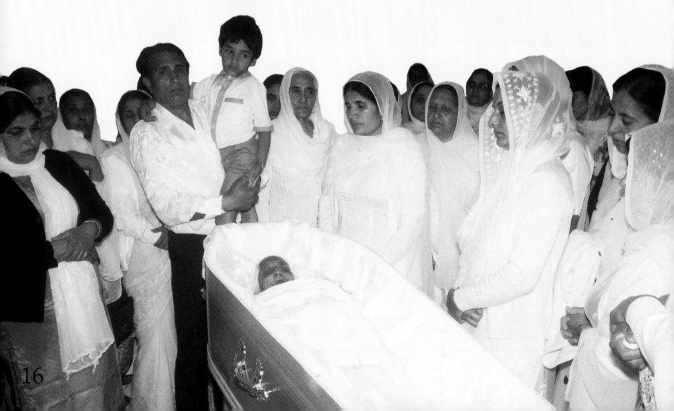

The coffin is taken to the gurdwara, the Sikh place of worship. Prayers are said outside the building. Afterwards, everyone returns to the gurdwara for more prayers and to share a meal. Sharing food with other Sikhs reminds the family that life must go on. It is traditional for **mourners** to give food or money to charity as a mark of respect for the person who has died.

For Sikhs who live in India, a dead person's ashes may be sprinkled in the holy river at Kiratpur in the Punjab. Elsewhere in the world, the ashes may be sprinkled in a river or the sea.

This is a gurdwara in the UK, and is where the coffin is taken and prayers are said.

Hindu funerals

Hindus believe in **reincarnation**. This means they do not believe that death is the end of life, but rather the start of a new life. They believe the person's **soul** goes to live within a new living being. So each person may have thousands of lives in this world. They also believe that if someone has lived a good life, then their next life may be happier.

Because of their belief in reincarnation, Hindus see the body of a dead person as something that is no longer needed after death. That is why a dead person's body is burnt on a fire, called a pyre, at a Hindu funeral. Sometimes, the funeral is held at a crematorium, but at a traditional Hindu funeral, pyres are usually built beside a river. This is because Hindus believe that running water is **holy** and cleansing.

The River Ganges in India is considered especially holy. There are pyre sites all along it.

A family scattering ashes into the river at Kiratpur, India.

The funeral usually happens on the day that the person has died. First the dead person's body is washed, if possible with water from the River Ganges. Then it is carried in a **procession** to the place of the pyre.

The dead person's son, or another male relative, walks around the pyre seven times. Then he lights the fire with a burning torch. A priest chants verses from the holy book, the Bhagavad Gita (say 'buh-guh-vud gee-tuh'). Relatives and friends say prayers for the dead person's soul, or spirit, as it leaves the body during the fire.

After three days, relatives collect the ashes from the dead person's body. If they can, Hindus scatter the ashes in the River Ganges. If they cannot get there, they may scatter the ashes in a river or the sea in their own country or region.

Air and sea burials

Sometimes, burial or **cremation** may be difficult, or forbidden for religious reasons. Other traditional ways of dealing with a dead person's body include air or sea burials.

Air burials

The **Zoroastrian** (say 'zo-roh-ass-tree-an-ism') religion started over 2500 years ago. According to Zoroastrian beliefs, a dead body should not be allowed to touch fire, earth or water, all of which are believed to be **holy**. So, instead, a dead person's body is cut into pieces and left in a high stone tower called a 'tower of silence' or dakhma. There, birds of prey, such as vultures, come for the flesh. Later, the bones are collected.

A similar ancient custom is still used in Tibet. Firewood is scarce, and so funeral pyres are very costly. At dawn, a dead person's body is carried to a remote hillside and left for birds and animals to finish off. For people who are used to these customs, they seem normal, and are no more upsetting than funerals in other cultures.

Towers of silence, or burial towers, in India. This is where a dead person's body is left.

A funeral service taking place on a ship. The person who has died will be buried at sea.

Sea burials

If someone dies on a long sea journey, or in a battle at sea, it may not be possible to carry their body back to land safely, without risking disease for other passengers. Then a sea burial may be the best option.

Some people today even choose a sea burial – perhaps if they have enjoyed sailing or holidays beside the sea.

For a sea burial, everyone gathers on the deck of the ship to remember the person who has died, and to say prayers or sing hymns or other songs. Then there is a respectful silence as the dead person's body is lowered into the sea, inside a **shroud** or coffin.

Remembering the dead

In Mexico, and some other Latin American countries, the Day of the Dead is marked every year on the 2 November. When someone dies, they are given a funeral, usually according to **Roman Catholic** tradition. But they are remembered especially on the Day of the Dead each year, a day set aside for the memory of those who have died.

The Day of the Dead began many hundreds of years ago, before Europeans brought **Christianity** to the USA. Many local traditions died out, but the Day of the Dead survived. Now it includes Catholic traditions as well.

People wearing fancy dress and skeleton masks in a procession for the Day of the Dead in Mexico.

In the days leading up to the Day of the Dead, people place flowers and gifts on their family graves, along with food and drinks – in case their relatives have grown hungry or thirsty in the grave.

On the day itself, there are great **processions** to the cemeteries. Families may spend the whole day at their relatives' graves, often bringing a picnic, and saying prayers for the dead.

A stall selling models of skulls and other grave decorations for the Day of the Dead.

Lorena's story

Lorena, a woman from Ecuador, remembers:

'My mother died when I was a girl. Every year on 2 November, my grandmother prepared avocado, chilli sauce and all my mother's favourite foods. We set out these foods, and left the window open all night so that she could come in and eat them. We knew that she didn't really come, but it is a way to remember someone who has died.'

Dancing at funerals

In many African countries, funerals are lively, with music, dancing and singing. Although relatives are sad at the loss of someone they loved, they do not see death as the end of life. Instead, death is celebrated as the way to the world of the **spirits**. Dancing and music reflect this joyful new life beginning – and also help those left behind to express their feelings.

At Yoruba funerals in Nigeria, West Africa, family and friends dance. They wear **symbolic** wooden masks, and there is drumming, singing and clapping. According to Yoruba beliefs, a dead person's spirit can still have control over his or her relatives. So it is very important to carry out the funeral and burial properly, in order to keep the spirit happy. Then it will help the living, instead of haunting them.

These men from the Dogon tribe are dancing on stilts at a funeral in Mali.

African people took their customs with them when they were forced to go as slaves to North and South America from the 16th to the 18th centuries. Some of these customs still survive today at funerals in communities of African origin in the USA and in Latin America. Often African traditions are combined with **Christian ritual**.

A jazz band playing in a funeral procession in New Orleans, USA.

One example is the jazz funeral of New Orleans, USA. Nowadays, these funerals are held mostly for jazz musicians. A jazz band plays as the coffin is brought in a **procession** to the church. At first, the band plays sad, marching music. There is a Christian funeral service in the church. But after the service, the band strikes up a joyous, jazzy sound and everyone dances their way back to a party, given in memory of the person who has died.

Ancestor worship

In China, as well as Japan, Vietnam and other countries in Asia, many people still follow the ancient traditions of **ancestor** worship. According to these beliefs, ancestors' **spirits** live on after death, and can affect the living.

Ancestor worship means that it is important to treat the dead person's body and spirit with respect at the funeral, and afterwards, too. This way, his or her spirit can rest in peace and bring good luck to the family left behind, instead of coming back to haunt them and bring bad luck.

These people are visiting their ancestors' graves in Tokyo, Japan.

Graves among the rice fields near Hanoi, Vietnam.

At the funeral, **mourners** may bring white or yellow flowers. The body is placed in an open coffin, with the feet facing the door. This encourages the dead person's soul to leave, rather than stay to haunt the living. Family and friends may offer **incense**, candles, tea, wine and food. Traditionally, everyone gives money to the relatives of the person who has died.

As the coffin is lowered into the grave, everyone turns away, as it is considered unlucky to watch this. Most families keep a month of mourning, when relatives and friends visit them at home, bringing gifts of food.

Visiting ancestors' graves

In China, at the spring festival of Qingming (say 'Ching-ming'), families visit the graves of their ancestors to sweep and tidy them. They bring picnics, and some of the food is offered to the ancestors in front of the grave. In return, they believe, ancestors will bring good health and wealth to the family. Then the rest of the food is enjoyed by the family.

New and old traditions

Many people nowadays do not follow any religion. Their relatives and friends may plan a new kind of funeral without prayers or religious readings. Other people look back to ancient **pagan** traditions that started before **Christianity**.

Pagans holding hands in a circle, surrounded by trees.

Humanists are a group of people who do not pray to a god, but instead value the life of every human being. Humanist funerals celebrate the memory of the person who has died, and all that he or she did during life, without religious **ritual**. Humanists accept that death is simply the end of life.

According to ancient pagan tradition, trees were a **symbol** of the cycle of life, producing seeds to make new life in a never-ending cycle. Modern day pagans celebrate funerals among trees or woodland, holding hands to make a circle as a symbol of the cycle of life.

Some people choose a green burial: that is, burial in a grave marked by planting a tree instead of a gravestone. Then green woodland can grow as a **memorial** for those who have died. More and more green burial grounds are being created as more people choose this kind of burial.

At this green burial in Devon, UK, a decorated cardboard coffin is being used.

Myra's story

Myra was grown up when her mother died. Here she remembers her mother's non-religious funeral:

'When our mother died, we wanted the people who had loved her to lead her funeral. We asked her two dearest friends to speak about her life. Then my sister and I talked about our memories of her. Another friend chose music that my mother had loved when she was alive. Thinking about what to say at her funeral helped me to appreciate what she had given to us, her family and friends.'

Glossary

ancestor relative in the past. Your grandparents and great-grandparents are your ancestors.

Buddhists (Buddhism) people who follow the way of life taught by the Buddha, who lived in ancient India. The Buddha was not a god, but a man. He taught his followers how to live simple, peaceful lives.

burial when a dead person's body is placed in a grave and covered with earth

Christians (Christianity) people who follow the religion of Christianity, which is based on the teachings of Jesus Christ. Christians believe that Jesus was the Son of God.

cremation when a dead person's body is burned

Hindus (Hinduism) people who follow Hinduism. Hindus worship one god (called Brahman) in many forms. Hinduism is the main religion in India.

holy special because it is to do with God or a religious purpose

incense a substance that gives a sweet smell when burnt and is sometimes used in religious rituals

Jews (Judaism) people who follow the religion of Judaism. Jews pray to one god.

memorial to honour and remember the person who has died

mourn feel or express sadness that a person has died

Muslims (Islam) people who follow the religion of Islam. Muslims pray to one god, whom they call Allah.

Orthodox strict or traditional

pagan someone who does not follow any of the main religions, but instead sees the natural world as holy

pilgrimage journey taken for religious reasons

procession people walking together along a route as part of a public or religious festival

reincarnation belief that after death, each person starts a new life on earth as another living thing

Roman Catholics Christians who follow the leadership of the Pope in Rome

shroud light sheet that is wrapped around a dead body before burial

Sikhs (Sikhism) people who follow the religion of Sikhism, based on the teachings of the ten Gurus, or teachers

soul/spirit the non-physical, spiritual part of a person, which some people believe survives after death

symbol/symbolic when a picture or object stands for something else

urn vase used to store the ashes of the dead

Zoroastrians (Zoroastrianism) people who follow the religion of Zoroastrianism. They live in India, where they fled from Persia (modern Iran) in the 8th century. Zoroastrians worship one god, and believe that the world is a struggle between good and evil.

Further resources

Ceremonies and Celebrations: Life's End, Denise Chaplin (Hodder Wayland, 2001)

Lifetimes, Bryan Mellonie (Belitha Press, 1997)

Life Times: Journey's End, Anita Ganeri (Evans, 1998)

Peoples and Customs of the World: Rites of Passage, Jacqueline Dineen (Conari Press, 1996)

Index

African traditions 24–5
afterlife 5, 8, 10, 12
air burials 20
Allah 8, 9
ancestor worship 26–7
anniversaries 7, 15

Buddhist funerals 14–15
burial 4, 5, 6, 9, 11, 13, 27, 29

cemeteries 9, 13
Christian funerals 12–13
coffins 6, 8, 9, 12, 14, 16, 17, 21, 27
cremation 4, 5, 6, 9, 13, 14, 16, 18, 19
cycle of life 14, 28

dancing and singing 24–5
Day of the Dead 22–3

God 6, 8, 12
gravestones 7, 11
green burials 29

Hindu funerals 18–19
holy writings 6, 8, 12, 14, 16, 19
humanist funerals 28

jazz funerals 25
Jewish funerals 6–7

Maori funerals 10–11
meals and parties 7, 11, 13, 17, 23, 25, 27
mourners 7, 9, 13, 17, 27
Muslim funerals 8–9

non-religious funerals 28–9

pagan traditions 28
prayers 6, 7, 8, 9, 12, 15, 17, 19, 21
processions 4, 5, 8, 12, 14, 19, 23, 25
pyres 15, 18, 19

reincarnation 5, 14, 18
respect for the dead 6, 10, 17, 26
rites of passage 4
rituals 4
Roman Catholics 13, 22

scattering the ashes 13, 17, 19
sea burials 21
shrouds 6, 9, 21
Sikh funerals 16–17
soul or spirit 4, 5, 8, 10, 11, 12, 14, 16, 18, 19, 24, 26, 27

transmigration 16

washing the body 4, 5, 9, 14, 16, 19

Zoroastrian tradition 20